GET OVER IT!

47 TIPS FOR EMBRACING THE DISCOMFORT OF CHANGE

One a week...almost, because you need a few weeks off. Change is hard, for crying out loud!

ANNE BONNEY

Editor: Ken Wachsberger
Cover Photo: Sarah Brown Photography
Design for Cover/Interior: Kendra Cagle

ISBN: 978-0-578-59079-0

www.AnneBonney.com

Dedication

To my parents, Al and Joan Bonney.
I never questioned your love for
me, and that has given me wings.

TABLE OF CONTENTS

INTRODUCTION

OK, LET'S FACE IT.
SOMETIMES CHANGE SUCKS.

We liked the way it was, we don't know what's going to happen, we don't agree with it, or it's just scary, even though we know it's good for us. Well, I've got some strategies for you.

But instead of a big book to take up more of your time, let's make this book digestible because we're all moving fast and often don't have time to sit down in the window with a cup of tea and a cat on our lap and read. (But boy that sounds nice right now!) So, how about a tip a week! Leave this on your nightstand, or coffee table. (Or in the magazine rack by your toilet. Seriously! Sometimes that's the only place we can get a little peace and quiet, for crying out loud!) Grab it when you need a spark of courage to get through whatever change is being thrust your way and marinate on that thought while you move on with your day.

Go get 'em, Tiger!

THE 5 P's

OF GETTING THROUGH

CHANGE

There is a system here, I go through it in detail in my keynotes and workshops, but this isn't a workshop. This is a quick-and-dirty tactical manual to help you get through whatever is changing in your life. Here's a quick overview of the 5 Ps, which comprise the five sections of this book.

1. Point
What the point? Why is this happening?

2. Problem
What is your problem? What is causing all the discomfort?

3. Path
How are we going to get through this?

4. Punch it, Margaret!
Time to go! Put the pedal to the metal and move forward!

5. Persevere
This is the fun part. (That's sarcasm!) Keep doing it. Keep going. It's not new and shiny anymore. Keep your eye on the prize and, as my pal Dory said, "Just keep swimming."

TIP 1

WHAT'S
THE
POINT?

OK. SO, SOMETHING IS CHANGING.

Maybe you decided to make the change, maybe you saw it coming, or maybe it dropped on your head like a piano out of a 10th floor window. Whatever the case, something is different, and you're uncomfortable about it. Best thing to do is identify why it's changing.

- **If you chose it, why are you making the change?**
- **If you didn't choose it, why is it happening?**

Getting clear here will help you stay the course when the road gets bumpy. So take a sec and do a little brain drain on why this is all happening. And sometimes the answer is, "Cuz life happens." and that's the best you're gonna get!

WHY GOD WHY????

TIP 2

RELAX!

IT'S NOT

ALL

CHANGING

Often when something changes, we go overboard with the magnitude of the disaster. Usually if we take a sec to think about what's actually changing, and what isn't changing, we can grab onto a little perspective and realize it's not as bad as we're making it out to be.

SO, TAKE A FEW MINUTES TO NOODLE WHAT IS CHANGING, AND WHAT ISN'T.

WHAT'S CHANGING?

WHAT'S NOT CHANGING?

TIP 3

FIND OUT

WHAT'S

FERRRRREAL

Many times we get all bent up because something in changing. We jump to conclusions and make assumptions that actually aren't true! Before you go off the deep end, take some time to be sure you fully understand what's going on. If this is a change at work, ask some questions, CALMLY! Things are rarely as bad as we think at first, so be sure to get the full picture.

DON'T LET SUSPICIOUS CONCLUSIONS RUIN YOUR DAY. LET THE DOWN-AND-DIRTY FACTS DO THAT!

TIP 4

Focus

ON WHAT YOU

CAN CONTROL

WE ALL LIKE CONTROL, BUT THERE IS A LOT WE CAN'T CONTROL.

(Sorry, all you control freaks out there, it's true. But stick with me here. You'll like where this ends up!)

Many times when we don't like a change, we freak out, dig our heels in, and refuse to budge, even when the change is inevitable and out of our control. Digging in your heels only wears out your shoes, leaves ruts in the ground, and ruins your day. (And the days of everyone around you.) I don't know about you, but I have plenty to put my energy towards where I can actually have an impact. I don't want to waste my time and energy (and intelligence) on something I can't control. So, take a deep breath, and identify what you have no control over. You might as well just get on that freight train and make the ride as enjoyable as possible…for everyone!

You still may not like it…and that's ok! We'll get to that in a bit.

"We can't control the winds, but we can adjust the sails."
—RICKY SKAGGS, 15-TIME GRAMMY-WINNING COUNTRY SINGER

TIP 5

FIND
THE
SILVER LINING

My friend Leila calls me "PollyAnna" because I'm always finding the silver lining. Heck, when something is changing, and you don't have any control over it, you might as well find the good in it, right? I mean, all you really have control over is how you react to what happens. You can choose to be miserable, or you can choose to look at the silver lining.

HELPFUL TIP:

THIS EXERCISE OFTEN REQUIRES A BOTTLE OF WINE, AN OPEN-MINDED FRIEND WHO IS WILLING TO PLAY ALONG, AND HONESTLY, A LITTLE SARCASTIC HUMOR.

First, make a list of all the things you hate about the change. Even if you're choosing it, there are always things that you're dreading, so go crazy! All the things you despise. All of 'em. Even the little stuff. Then, ball it up and burn it! Then make a list of all the positives. This is where the sarcastic humor comes in, because sometimes you really have to reach and come up with things that may seem silly, like, say you get laid off, which sucks! A few silver linings… "I won't have to work with that terrible boss anymore!" and "I won't have to smell Smiddy's microwaved fish lunches anymore!" Get silly, get ridiculous, but challenge yourself to come up with at least 20 things! Seriously. It's actually kinda fun if you let yourself get into it. Keep that list, and refer to it when your outlook starts to swirl to the dark side!

PAINT

YOUR

LIGHTHOUSE

YOU'RE IN THE CHANGE.
EVERYTHING IS UNCOMFORTABLE.
YOU'RE MISERABLE INSIDE.

IF YOU CHOSE IT, YOU'RE SERIOUSLY CONSIDERING GOING BACK. IF YOU DIDN'T, YOU'RE JUST PISSED, BLAMING PEOPLE FOR YOUR MISERY AND CRUSHING AN *Oscar*-WORTHY PERFORMANCE AS "*Victim* #1."

Ok, that's enough of that. Time to look into your crystal ball. If you want to make it a whole lot easier on yourself emotionally, put on your rose-colored glasses and paint a picture of the future. Whether it's a week, a month, or a year from now (or longer), predict when the change will be the new status quo. What's happening at that time? What are the benefits? How are you feeling? Imagine the best-case scenario when things are all settled down. Maybe calm and ease return, or if you're an entrepreneur who left a six-figure income job to start your own business, maybe it's the phone ringing off the hook, you hiring a team, and jet setting all over the world to ink massive business deals. However your bright future looks, imagine it. Then keep that image in your head when the road gets rough, and keep moving toward it.

TIP 7

DON'T
DO IT
ALONE

As humans, we have a strong need to connect, and one of the most difficult things in life is feeling like you're alone. I've got news for you. YOU'RE NOT! Even though it may fit beautifully with your paradigm of downtrodden victim (if that's your style), the fact is, all that point of view does is make you more miserable. Reach out. Who do you know who has gone through this type of transition before? Who can share some coping techniques? Who can give you some tips?

WHO CAN JUST LISTEN AND SAY, "WOW! THAT REALLY SUUUUUCKS! I KNOW WHAT YOU'RE DEALING WITH."

WHATEVER CONNECTION YOU NEED TO HELP YOU GET THROUGH WHATEVER CHANGE YOU'RE DEALING WITH, GO FIND IT.

And if you reach out, and someone doesn't respond, don't freak out. No malice, they just may not be the one to help you at that moment. Ask someone else. Find your people. You would do the same for them. Seriously. And, heck, these days, it can even be with a bunch of strangers on the Internet, or in a meetup group! If you don't think your current circle is equipped to help you, widen your circle! It takes about eight seconds of courage, but you'll find that people really want to help. DO IT!

TIP 8

What's
YOUR
PROBLEM???

Now we're on to the second *P* of this magical, five-*P* journey into change. Isn't this fun?

Ok, so now it's time to go inside and explore why the heck you're getting so bent about this. (And please note: It's totally normal and fine to get bent. We all do it. You're human. I do it, and I wrote this book!) The key is not to get hung up by your initial emotional reaction. It is a common problem. People get stuck in an emotional state and don't move on. Part of developing emotional intelligence (which is MASSIVELY important) is to examine your emotions and be able to regulate them.

SO, LET'S DIVE IN!

TIP 9

ACKNOWLEDGE
YOUR
FEELINGS

FEELINGS ARE OK!

In fact, they're completely normal and human. So maybe you're angry. Maybe you're sad. Scared? Absolutely. That's ok!! Your feelings are yours and valid, and often they are negative when dealing with change. (Otherwise this would be a very different book: *Ain't Change Great: Embracing the Joy of Sudden and Undesired Change!* But it's not!) Acknowledge how you feel, because your feelings are legitimate. They're your feelings. You can't help it. Now, how you choose to ACT as a result of those feelings, that's where we separate the victims from the superheroes! You have the power to decide how you respond.

But first, take some time to acknowledge how you feel. Write it out. This is no time to edit. Feel it. Be bratty. Be negative. This is your chance. VENT! It never has to go beyond this page. It's just for you so pour it on out there. (You might need more paper!)

I FEEL . . . _____

_____

_____

_____

_____

TIP 10

IDENTIFY

YOUR

DISCOMFORT

Once you've identified your feelings, it's good to think about why you feel that way. What are the reasons for your feelings? Because once you know why you're feeling a certain way, you are better able to think of a way to ease those feelings. For example, are you scared of the unknown of this change because you like to have a plan and know what's going to happen? Make a list of what's in your control and think about those. Are you sad because of what you're losing? Make a list of what you're gaining and keep those in mind. Get it?

WRITE OUT WHY YOU'RE FEELING
THE WAY YOU ARE.

I FEEL . . . _____

_____

_____

BECAUSE . . . _____

_____

SIDENOTE: THIS IS A FUN EXERCISE TO DO IN ONE OF THOSE PLACES WHERE THEY LET YOU BREAK THINGS! YOU CAN SCREAM OUT THE REASONS FOR YOUR FEELINGS WHILE SMASHING TELEVISIONS AND GLASSWARE WITH A BASEBALL BAT. THAT TIP ALONE IS WORTH THE PRICE OF THIS BOOK!

TIP 11

DON'T WALLOW...

IT'S SO

OVERDONE

OK, ALL THIS VENTING IS FINE AND GOOD, BUT AT SOME POINT, IT'S TIME TO MOVE ON! SERIOUSLY.

It's not easy, you won't be ready, and you'll hate it, but life goes on, and you must, too! So, wallow, cry, stomp your feet, have your hissy fit, and then move on. And don't wait too long, ok? Because your friends will get sick of your whiney crap! Sometimes it helps to set yourself a deadline. Allow yourself to wallow and mourn the passing of the past, with the understanding that in five days you're going to start moving forward. Also, it's good to think about what your first act of onwardness is going to be, so you have a distinct action to kick off your forward charge.

THE DATE I WILL MAKE MY FIRST GET OVER IT ACTION:

_____

THAT ACTION IS:

_____

_____

_____

TIP 12

Take a Walk
DOWN
MEMORY LANE

Close your eyes for a moment. Shoot. You can't read when you close your eyes. Ok, open them, but think back. You've dealt with change before. What helped you get through it last time? Maybe it wasn't as dramatic of a change. Maybe it was a long time ago. Maybe the change was completely different but trying what has worked for you in the past is definitely worth a try.

GIVE IT A SHOT.

A PAST BIG CHANGE I HAD TO DEAL WITH WAS:

_____

_____

_____

WHEN THAT HAPPENED, THIS HELPED ME THROUGH:

_____

_____

_____

_____

TIP 13

WRITE YOURSELF

SOME

SASSY BACKTALK

Any time you're between comfort zones, that inner voice in your head will remind you of the worst-case scenario, of how great it used to be, of how you can always go back to what's easy and what you know. It tries to get you to go back to where you were because it can't see where you're going.

You know the voice I'm talking about. It's loud, it's mean, and it lies, but it lies really well and many people believe it. Well, not you, my friend. You're getting over it and marching to that new comfort zone. (And you're darned uncomfortable until you get there!) What you need is something to tell that inner jerk when it starts lying to you. Some people call it a mantra; others call it an affirmation. I like to call it an argument so you can tell that inner voice where to go because it's wrong. Once you have that argument statement, you need to intentionally repeat it to yourself to flex those courage muscles when the inner jerk starts squawking.

MAKE IT SHORT AND PEPPY AND STRONG.

WHEN MY INNER JERK STARTS SQUAWKING, I'M GOING TO SAY :

_____

_____

_____

_____

TIP 14

WHO YOU
GONNA
CALL?

MISERY LOVES COMPANY.
OK, I'M KIDDING...KINDA.

As my friend Shea says, "Healing happens through networking." Someone else has been through what you're going through, and they may have the perfect answer. Don't try to go through it alone. But don't go to that friend who will just "yes" you to death. You need someone who can truly understand your discomfort, and has experience getting beyond it. Talk to them. Learn from them. They can help you set realistic expectations and develop strategies that worked for them. At the very least, they'll give you validation that your feelings are totally legit and reassure you that everything is going to be ok. Sometimes you need that voice of experience to talk you off the ledge when you're freaking out.

MAKE A LIST OF POSSIBLE SUPPORT STAFFERS.

_____

_____

_____

_____

_____

_____

TIP 15

WHAT'S
MY
PATH?

Time to move forward and get on with the getting over it! Figuring out what your plan is will help you persevere once you get started, so take the time to think about how you're going to tackle this thing. It'll change along the way, so it might be a complete waste of time, but you'll feel a lot more confident diving in if you at least have a few steps laid out for yourself.

(I'M KIDDING ABOUT THE WASTE OF TIME... KINDA. WELCOME TO LIFE.)

TIP 16

DON'T BE A BULL
IN A
CHINA SHOP

How much fun is it to hang out with that friend who is constantly moaning and whining about something? (Sometimes it's even something they created themselves!) It's no fun at all.

SO DON'T BE "THAT GUY"! COME ON. YOU'RE BETTER THAN THAT!

Now that you're taking on this change, whether you chose it or not, make the decision to handle it gracefully! Ok, so maybe you don't like it. Sure, you didn't pick it, but once you're at this point of planning how you're going to get through it, you have to decide how you're going to handle the tough times. Journal? Meditation? Ice cream? Happy hour with a friend? (Note: I said HAPPY hour!)

Figure out how you're going to deal with yourself when you're feeling down. That doesn't mean you can't call a friend (or therapist) and talk through your challenge, but don't call everyone you know to talk through it, and, god forbid, don't post something cryptic and depressing on social media. That's just pitiful.

TIP 17

WHO HAS TRAVELED THIS PATH BEFORE?

YOU'RE NOT ALONE.

As good as it feels sometimes to wallow in the melodrama of "woe is me" and "I'm the only one who understands my pain," it's time to graduate from middle school and adult-up already. You're not alone, your situation is not unique.

That doesn't mean it sucks any less, but it does mean that you don't have to plan this alone. Reach out to that friend/acquaintance/stranger on a street corner who you vented to in tip 14 *(Who you gonna call?)* and ask them to help you find the path. Buy them a hamburger and ask them to share how they did it. (...or kale if they're on a diet but be warned: People eating kale aren't as open with the information because they're too busy being angry that they're eating kale.)

WHO CAN HELP ME WITH THE HOW?

_____

_____

WHEN WILL I CALL THEM?
(SERIOUSLY, COMMIT TO A DATE AND TIME...RIGHT NOW!)

_____

_____

TIP 18

CONSIDER
THE
BIG MOVE

CONSIDER THE BIG MOVE.

For instance, if you have a new boss you really don't like, consider getting a new job. If you get laid off and you can't find another job in your industry, consider joining the circus. If your spouse announces his impending gender reassignment surgery, consider leaving the relationship. I'm not saying you should make the big change, but consider it.

The key is to think about what is within your control. Then, when you decide that the reasons to stick around are more compelling than the reasons to make the BIG MOVE, you have now chosen to stay, and you don't feel like as much of a victim of the situation. Or, you may find that you don't have enough reasons to stay, and it could mark the first day of the next amazing chapter that you never knew you always wanted.

"WE PUT A LOT OF EMPHASIS ON STAYING, AND SOMETIMES THE BEST CHOICE YOU CAN MAKE IS TO LEAVE."
—CAMILLE YAMEEN, IGNITING COURAGE PODCAST EPISODE 47

TIP 19

BREAK

IT

UP

HUGE FARAWAY GOALS ARE BIG
AND SEEM IMPOSSIBLE.

If you're changing your workout routine to eventually run a marathon and you have never run a mile, aiming for 26 miles will not be motivating. Aiming to run a 3 mile race first seems a lot more possible, more motivating! When you believe you can reach your goal, you're much more likely to reach for it. Same with getting a degree, or starting your own business, or implementing a new computer system at work. The end result may seem daunting, so break the journey into more believable steps so you feel successful as you're moving closer. So instead of planning to "start your own business," start with "launch my website" and "finish my business plan." That will give you progress that you can feel good about as you march toward that big change.

TIP 20

ONE BITE
AT A
TIME

HOW DO YOU EAT AN ELEPHANT?
ONE BITE AT A TIME.

Baby, you need some milestones, because when you reach them you're going to get a massage.

I mean seriously, this is hard, and you deserve a little celebration! Select a few milestones, maybe pretty close together at first, and decreasing in frequency as you gain momentum and start seeing results, but pick those milestones. I like to call them "The Cork Popping Moments" when you can take a break, sip some bubbly, and give yourself a pat on the back. This is especially important if you're not particularly excited about the change. Build in some "pat yourself on the back" milestones, so it's not all "AARGH, look how much farther I have to go!" This is a great time to pull in your accountability partner/coach so they can sip the bubbly with you.

TIP 21

GIVE YOURSELF
A
DEADLINE

KNOW YOUR TIMELINE.
WHEN DOES THIS CHANGE NEED TO BE IN PLACE? WHEN DO I WANT IT TO BE IN PLACE?

I'm a believer in "rip off the Band-Aid". Put a date on it. Commit to a completion date. Figure out how much leeway you're going to give yourself, and when it will be time to charge full-speed ahead. A deadline will create urgency and keep you moving forward, even when you don't want to move anywhere, so figure out your timeline. I even put the milestones on my calendar. They may change, but again, I'm trying to create a sense of urgency for myself, because otherwise I kick in some next level procrastination and end up with zero progress. You get me?

TIP 22

BACK IT UP

AND

GET REAL

WHEN TRYING TO MOVE THROUGH A CHALLENGING CHANGE,
MANY OF US WILL GET ALL "SHOOT FOR THE MOON!" WHEN WE'RE
CREATING OUR TIMELINES AND MILESTONES, BUT COME ON.

We have all experienced how demoralizing it is to watch our spectacular stretch goal fade into the distance as real life clamps its ball and chain to our ankles. Time to be realistic about how much you can fit into your already crammed full life, whether you like it or not. You will exponentially increase your chances of continued motivation. Remember that you simply may not have enough time in the day for family, full-time job, personal hygiene, sleep, eating, AND getting your degree in under two years, so be realistic.

YOU'LL THANK YOURSELF LATER.

TIP 23

TIME TO LIGHTEN
YOUR
LOAD

During times of big change, tons of emotions will show up for the party. Fear, anger, sadness, maybe some excitement. But with all those feelings comes your old pal Overwhelm! You may have a lot to do, or a lot that's demanding your focus and energy, so how can you simplify your life? Saying no is a great thing to do at times like this. Asked to volunteer for something? Now may not be the right time. Maybe this is a time to hire someone to clean your house, so you don't have to do it. Or order a month or two of Blue Apron, saving yourself grocery shopping and menu planning. (I love Blue Apron! Seriously! Thank you!) How can you simplify your life? Because maybe this is the season to do it.

YOU'RE A MUCH BETTER SUPERHERO WHEN YOU DELEGATE THE LITTLE STUFF TO SOMEONE ELSE...OR JUST DELEGATE IT FOR LATER!

TIP 24

RIGHT-SIZE
YOUR
EXPECTATIONS

Most challenges and conflicts in life are due to unrealistic or unclear expectations. I truly believe the key to happiness is right-sizing your expectations.

SO, WHAT ARE YOUR EXPECTATIONS OF YOURSELF?

If you're someone who hates change, and it always takes you a long time to get over it, give yourself some time. Maybe a little less than last time, but don't expect a herculean change in your ability to Get Over It! Maybe you want to be the kind of person who is able to just shrug and get on with brunch, but you're you, your sparkles and your warts! So, aim for a little improvement, and celebrate when you nail that. Unrealistic expectations will just make you feel unsuccessful, frustrated, and disappointed in yourself, and you don't need that in your life right now.

TIP 25

SAY It
OUT
LOUD

OK, IT'S TIME TO GRAB THAT ADDRESS BOOK AGAIN AND HIT UP YOUR SUPPORT PERSON!

TIME TO GET THEM INVOLVED IN YOUR PLAN.

It may be for feedback, maybe accountability, or maybe it's just to say "Here's what I'm doing" so they can enthusiastically exclaim, "YES! You've got this. You're gonna be great!" This someone may not be the guru who's trod the path before. This is your rainbow-farting, glitter-burping, bouncing, joyful friend who will fill you with sunshine and positive energy whenever you need it. We need these people in our lives. The ones who live by the motto, "What would Richard Simmons do?" If you're not a hugger, and you identify more with grumpy cat, they're a little annoying, but you can't help but love those happy little dipshits. (As a founding member of the Happy Little Dipshit Coalition, I can say that.)

TIP 26

WRITE
IT
DOWN

This may seem like a wasted step, but as you're setting goals for your progress toward comfort in your new reality, write it down. Like, with a pen. On a piece of paper. With your hand. Not your fingers on a keyboard but, with a real live pen. (A pencil will do…and a pencil with a hairy-topped troll doll on the top will work even better!) Just the act of writing it down will give you a better chance of achieving it. Seriously. It's like science and stuff! Ask Dr. Gail Matthews of Dominican University of California. She did a study with 270 people and found that those who wrote down their goals were 42% more likely to achieve them. A Harvard Biz Study found that the 3% of MBA students who wrote down their goals upon graduation were earning ten times more than the other 97% of their class ten years later! So seriously. If it's good enough for Harvard, it's good enough for you.

GET A PEN.
WRITE YOUR GOAL.

HERE'S A PLACE. Oooooo...PAPER. COOL!

TIP 27

THE FIRST STEP
IS
EVERYTHING!

THIS. IS. KEY.

WHAT IS THE FIRST ACTION YOU'RE GOING TO TAKE?

The scary part is, when you've got a long road ahead, sometimes this first action is the ONLY one you know of when you take it. Once you take that step, you start a domino effect, and your brain goes into achievement overdrive, so during this path-finding phase, identify that first step. Dream about it. Envision it going right. Sing about it. I don't care what you do, but identify it and get ready…set…

"A JOURNEY OF A THOUSAND MILES BEGINS WITH A SINGLE STEP."
—CONFUCIOUS

TIP 28

PUNCH IT,
MARGARET!

SO IT'S TIME TO ACT! GO! DO! NOW!!!

It's not going to be comfortable. You're not going to be ready. You're going to want to crawl in bed and pull the covers over your eyes and binge watch some show you don't even give a crap about while eating a whole tube of cookie dough. But you're not going to do that because you're getting over it, and you can't get over it while you're wallowing. It. Just. Doesn't. Happen. So, go to tip 27 (The First Step is Everything!) and DO THAT!

NOW!
GO!

SERIOUSLY! 3...2...1...

TIP 29

ACTION
SHRIVELS
ANXIETY

WHEN YOU FEEL YOURSELF STARTING TO FREAK OUT ABOUT A CHANGE, DO SOMETHING!

Action will weaken the anxiety just like that sparkly green stuff weakens Superman. We all thought he was invincible, but NO. Same with anxiety.

When you're doing, you're taking action toward your goal. When I start freaking out about my speaking business not being exactly where I want it to be, I do some marketing, or I practice my keynote. If you're anxious about the new town you just moved to, take a walk, or go to the coffee shop and talk to the barista. Just…do…SOMETHING to move yourself toward your new comfort zone.

You might not feel like it. You might not feel like doing anything. The problem is, if you stay all anxious and wilty, your life will devolve into a three-day Hallmark Movie marathon with you in dirty sweats with Cheeto dust on your fingers, and a puddle of used tissues on the floor. Come on, Tiger. You're better that that!

"Ain't nobody got time for that."

—KIMBERLY "SWEET BROWN" WILKINS BEING INTERVIEWED AFTER HAVING ESCAPED A FIRE IN AN APARTMENT COMPLEX

TIP 30

YOU WON'T SEE THE
WHOLE PICTURE...
START ANYWAY

LIFE IS FULL OF UNKNOWNS.

For those of us who love to have the death grip on control, that part of change really stinks, but it's the reality. You are not going to be able to see the whole path to your new comfort zone. Or maybe you can, and then something will happen, and there will be a sharp turn to the left (usually in Albuquerque) and suddenly you have no idea how you're going to get there. The path to success is never straight. It's foggy and scary but look down. You can usually see the next step.

TAKE THAT STEP.

START!

The power of STARTING is incredible. Plus, if you never start, there's NO WAY you'll ever get there. So, take a deep breath and go, even if you don't have everything planned out. Believe me, you'll figure it out.

THIS IS THE FUN PART!

Ok, I'm totally lying. This is the really crappy, dull, hard part where that inner voice really starts to squawk and the desire to quit is strong. (Well, that's uplifting. Isn't it?) But have no fear. You can do this. You've done the pre-work. Now it's time to work the plan.

"MAY THE ODDS BE EVER IN YOUR FAVOR."

— EFFIE TRINKET, THAT CREEPY PINK-HAIRED LADY IN THE HUNGER GAMES

TIP 32

It's ABOUT

SMALL

DAILY STEPS

LET'S BE HONEST,
THIS PERSEVERING THING SUCKS.

ESPECIALLY WHEN YOU HAVE A LONG WAY TO GO TO YOUR NEW COMFORT ZONE.

It's often hard to have a sense of urgency when your goal is a long way off or seems so hard that it feels out of your reach. The key is, once you've got your plan, be sure you break it down into the daily tasks that you can do every day to reach your goal.

Writing a book seemed like a massive task for me until I made a commitment to write 500 words a day. That was a nice, easy fifteen-minute nugget, and by the end of one month, I had written over 15,000 words, a much more sizable chunk than when I was freaking out and not doing anything! So, figure out what little thing you can do every day to move yourself forward. Tiny steps forward are better than terrified stagnation!

TIP 33

JUST WORRY

ABOUT

TODAY

Someone said this to me once, and it floored me. Use it when you're thinking about a daunting future that you didn't choose, or you're choosing a path that's going to be really tough. For example, say your spouse suddenly left you and you're facing the prospect of *the rest of your life* alone. Or maybe you want to get down to a healthy weight, and realize that you have to cut way back on sugar in order to do that, and you're facing the prospect of *the rest of your life* without your delicious bowl of Mississippi Mudslide every night during the 10 o'clock news.

Well, of course, if you focus on A FUTURE WITHOUT whatever it is you're dealing with, it's going to make dealing with the situation a lot more difficult. But you don't have to worry about the rest of your life.

JUST WORRY ABOUT TODAY. OKAY?

THINK ABOUT THAT.

TIP 34

GET SOMEONE
TO HOLD YOUR
FEET TO THE FIRE

Your accountability partner or coach might be someone going through a similar change as you. It might be a professional who has the skills to hold you accountable. Whatever the case, you don't have to go through it alone, and if you have someone to rely on in those weak moments, you'll feel a lot stronger.

Plus, sometimes you won't have the belief in your own abilities, so borrowing theirs will help. They'll also call you on your baloney, which can be super helpful when you're in "woe is me" mode. So get someone involved. Don't make it that friend who wants to tell you what you want to hear. That's not what you need. Get that brutal friend who you know will tell it like it is. This is the beauty of hiring someone. They're paid to be honest, not flattering.

IF YOU WANT EASY AND FLATTERY, YOU MIGHT AS WELL QUIT NOW. BUT YOU WON'T.

YOU'RE STRONGER THAN THAT.

TIP 35

REMIND
YOURSELF
WHY

Why are you doing this? What's the lighthouse? What's the nirvana you're aiming at once you're comfortable with this new reality? Keep reminding yourself of it. Imagine it. Close your eyes and bring it to your mind. Walk around in it. Revel in it. Feel how it feels there. What are you thinking? What is easier? What is better?

IMAGINE ALL THE GOOD STUFF ON THE OTHER SIDE OF THIS CHALLENGE.

DESCRIBE YOUR BEAUTIFUL NEW REALITY ON
THE OTHER SIDE OF THIS MESS:

_____

_____

_____

_____

_____

_____

_____

TIP 36

FORGIVE YOURSELF

FOR NOT BEING

PERFECT

FAILURE IS A PART OF LIFE. GET OVER IT!

So often we completely give up the farm when we have one slip up. When dieting, you have a few bites of cake at lunch, and you figure the whole day is gone so you grab a whole pizza and a gallon of Breyers on the way home.

NO! Have the cake. Take your bites, beat yourself up FOR A SECOND, and then laugh, remind yourself you're human, and like all humans you're not perfect, but you can restart NOW! Jump right back on. Revel in the deliciousness of that little slip and move back into your plan. Give yourself a break, Shirley. It ain't all that.

"PERFECTION IS NOT A HUMAN QUALITY."
— MOLLY KENNEDY, YOUTH SPEAKER AND SUPER FABULOUS CHICK!

TIP 37

LOOK BACK
AND SEE
HOW FAR YOU'VE COME

I ran the Antarctica Marathon in 2007. It is a 13-mile course that you complete twice to do the full 26.2-mile distance. At around miles 4 and 17, you have to climb a glacier. It is steep and slippery and a long half mile from the beach to the turnaround at the top.

On my second time up, I was so tired I would count ten steps forward and I would stop for ten seconds to catch my breath. I was taking the glacier ten steps at a time. I was taking forever and the top didn't seem to be getting any closer. (Kind of like the bottom of a bowl of spaghetti at that fabulous Italian restaurant you love: You never seem to make any progress!)

Finally, on one of my ten-second rests, I turned around and looked at the beach below me. I could hardly see the tiny figures of my fellow runners down there. I realized how far I had come, and I got a fabulous burst of energy. So often we just focus on how much farther we have to go.

Don't forget to stop every once in a while and look at how far you've come.

IT'S AN INCREDIBLE MOTIVATOR!

TIP 38

CRANK UP THE
VOLUME
ON YOUR
SASSY BACKTALK

When the initial energy of the PUNCH IT has worn off, and the band goes home, life in the Perseverance Zone gets pretty dull, and sometimes pretty dark. This is where that inner jerk gets really loud, and sometimes really mean.

Time to brush off that phrase you wrote in Tip 13 (Write sassy backtalk) and jack up the volume. There will be moments when you doubt yourself. Say that phrase. There will be moments when you want to quit. Repeat that phrase. There will be moments when you feel like it's too much. Say it again. Keep that sucker on repeat until you believe it. (Because you might not at first!) Write it on your mirror. Put an image of it on the home screen of your cell. Tattoo it backwards on your forehead.

Do whatever you need to do to remind yourself to stay the course.

IT'LL HELP KEEP YOU STRONG. I PROMISE.

TIP 39

Circle Up
WITH THE
CHEERLEADERS

This seems so cliché, but seriously! If you always hang around with negative people who point out how horrible life is, you're going to see all the horrible stuff. If you surround yourself with doubters, they will just amplifying the voice in your head that keeps reminding you of all the doubts. Awesome. Super constructive.

(THAT'S SARCASM!)

Instead, find your supporters. Vent to the cheerleaders who are going to give you hope and a swift kick in the butt when you're wallowing in the negatives. Identify the believers and people you can learn from. Seek out people who have been there and are now thriving and focus on how to get where they are! Use them as your beacon.

THE DOUBTERS, EVEN THOUGH THEY MAY JUST BE
TRYING TO KEEP YOU "SAFE" FROM FAILURE,
WILL ALSO KEEP YOU SAFE FROM SUCCESS.

WALLOW IN THAT!

TIP 40

Everyone
LOVES
REWARDS

Especially if change is hard, reward yourself for reaching milestones or doing the tough thing. Seriously! What would you like? A massage? Sushi dinner with your sweetie? A weekend away? Maybe it's just walking down the hall to have a few minutes of social time. The more you pair something positive with completing something scary or unpleasant, the less resistance you'll feel for the tough stuff. Obviously, you're not going to plan a weekend away just for a small task like making one prospecting call in your new job. Make the reward intensity match the task or milestone intensity, but be sure to give yourself a little something as you've earned it.

Take a sec to list a few rewards that you would enjoy in response to achievement. Please note: Be realistic. If you can't afford that two-week vacation in Bali, maybe don't put it on the list right now.

SMALL REWARDS	LARGE REWARDS
_____	_____
_____	_____
_____	_____
_____	_____
_____	_____

TIP 41

TEN-MINUTE
RULE

I LOVE THIS RULE AND USE IT
A LOT IN MY WRITING.

(SOMETIMES IT'S SCARY FOR ME TO COMMIT WORDS TO "PAPER.")

Here's what you do. When you need to do something that will take a bit of time and that you're DREADING, set an alarm for ten minutes and start. When the alarm goes off, if you're still dreading it and having a horrible time, you can stop! At least you got ten minutes done, and you can do it again another time.

More often than not, though, by the time that timer rings, you'll have created some momentum and you'll keep going, and often end up finishing the job. (This is 100% true for me.) When it comes to stuff we really don't want to do, the activation energy of just getting started is the hardest part. Set a timer and start. Again, at least you'll get ten minutes done, but more likely, you'll finish the entire banana.

TIP 42

DON'T
GET
HANGRY

As much as we hate to admit it, our mood, our ability to be strong in the face of a challenge, and our energy to persevere are very closely related to our healthy habits

I know that if I miss my morning workout, and start the day with bad nutrition, my discipline for the rest of the day is shot. I'm also a blubbering idiot when I'm dehydrated.

Be very intentional about your food, sleep, exercise and nutrition. Drinking plenty of water is pretty easy if you stop whining about how hard it is. Eat a salad instead of a burger. One less adult beverage perhaps, or decaf? (hangover and over-caffeination doesn't help anyone!) And you don't need a 2 hour daily sweatfest. Just use the stairs instead of the elevator, park farther away or have a walking meeting.

When you take care of yourself, you build up emotional fortitude to help quiet that internal jerk, quell that fear of failure, and stoke that fire of courage. Get to know yourself and what you've done when you're feeling strong and do that again!

AS MY GRANDMA SAID,
"IF IT AIN'T BROKE, DON'T FIX IT."

TIP 43

ESCAPE!

Is there something you love to do that
absorbs your attention.

FIND THE TIME TO DO THAT.

Taking time to get away from the stress and demands of persevering through this toughest phase of change will help create the energy to keep going. Make this a reward for taking a step or doing a "big scary." Is it yoga or meditation? The mosh pit at a metal concert? An outdoor activity or craft? Whatever it is, do it! Take the time to escape from the burden so, when you get back to it, you're refreshed and renewed. (for me, it's assembling IKEA furniture. I seriously love it. I get completely absorbed with trying to figure out where that last little bolt goes!)

TIP 44

FOR CRYING OUT LOUD,
STOP SAYING
YES

During the season of change, when you're elbow deep in stress and adaptation, maybe this is a time to not take on new stuff, and eliminate stressors that are creating more anxiety than good. In other words, say no.

SAY IT WITH ME:
"NO!"

Does that make you cringe? Try this:
"I'm sorry, but I won't be able to do that."

Still having a tough time? How about this one: "I'm sorry! I won't be able to do that right now." (The "right now" part can show that you're interested in helping, but right now isn't the time.)

Or, if you want to get really fancy: "I'm sorry, but with everything else I have going on right now, I wouldn't be able to do this to the quality that it deserves." Frankly, you're being 100% honest, and saying, "Look, if you want me to do a crappy, half-assed job, then I'm your huckleberry. Is that what you want?" The answer is always going to be "No," so give it a shot.

GO ON. YOU'LL BE OK!

Eat THAT FROG

Brian Tracy wrote a fantastic time management book called *Eat That Frog*. You know when there's something that you really don't want to do, and you've been avoiding, and bumping from today's to-do list, to tomorrow's, to tomorrow's, to tomorrow's, and it keeps staring at you and casting a dark shadow on your daily productivity.

Mr. Tracy's premise is, if you eat a live frog first thing in the morning, everything else that day isn't that bad. For the record, I'm willing to bet that Mr. T. has never actually eaten a LIVE frog. He's not being literal. The frog is that task you don't want to do. Make it THE FIRST thing you do on a given day. Eat the frog. First thing! Not only will you get it OFF the list, but you'll also create great momentum for the rest of the day. I love this strategy and use it often for tasks I am absolutely dreading.

PARTNER THIS WITH TIP 41 (10-MINUTE RULE).

"IF YOU HAVE TO SWALLOW A FROG, DON'T STARE AT IT TOO LONG"
— MARK TWAIN

TIP 46

Be flexible
AND
ADJUST

As you're working the plan, sometimes things don't go so well. Sometimes we learn things and realize the plan was terrible. As you go, periodically reflect on the plan and adjust it. It's nice to have a path that's set in stone, but such a plan is not realistic.

WE LEARN AS WE GO, SO REFLECT AND ADJUST AS NEEDED.

Oh, and don't forget to reflect on the things that go right. Pat yourself on the back and plan to keep doing those things

TIP 47

SETTLE IN
AND
GIVE IT TIME

As you're traveling your path and persevering like the champion that you are, you will hit speed bumps . Things sometimes won't work, or will seem like they're not working. Be sure to give strategies time to work. Before you abandon one, ask yourself, "Does this not work, or has it not worked YET."

When you're changing the way you relate to someone else, it often takes time for the trust to build, so you might have to keep at it. When you're trying to lose weight, and you've got a plan you were pretty excited about, be sure you don't give up if you haven't lost the weight of your left leg in the first three days. (Seriously, that's not realistic people. Don't believe those skinny people on the Internet. They're not real.)

Don't get discouraged until you have truly given something the time it deserves to work.

CHANGE TAKES TIME AND PATIENCE AND PERSEVERANCE, SO SETTLE IN AND GIVE IT A CHANCE.

BONUS TIP

FINAL

THOUGHTS

Well my friends, that's it. I wish I could say that having read this book, you're now going to be an amazing ninja of change-acceptance. I'd love to blow glitter up your butt and make you believe that, but, I can't. It doesn't work that way and I love you too much to lie to you.

Now starts the work. Pick a tip a week and intentionally put it into action. You've got a ton going on every day and can only really focus on one personal development adventure at a time, so pick one that really spoke to you, and focus on only that one until it becomes a little more normal. Like I said in Tip 36 (Forgive yourself), you're going to mess it up. The way you learn is to catch yourself, figure out what you're going to do next time, and charge ahead. Every time you catch yourself slipping back to old habits, and plan your adjustment, you'll be one step closer to it being the new habit. It could take 3 catches, it could take 30. Everyone is different, but stick with it kid.

IT'S ALL ABOUT THE JOURNEY!

GOOD LUCK!

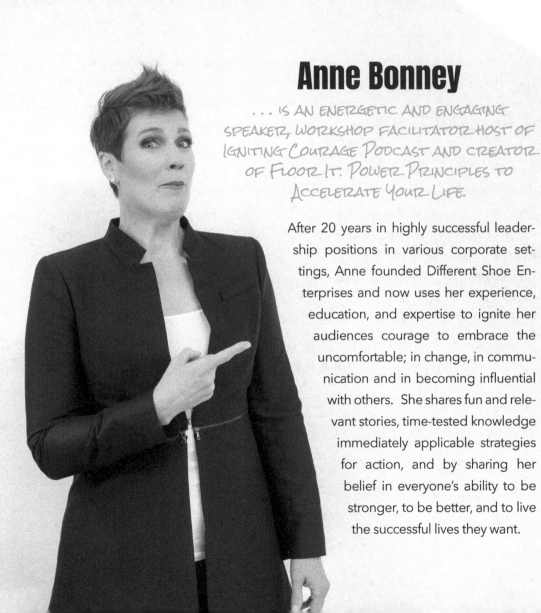

Anne Bonney

. . . IS AN ENERGETIC AND ENGAGING SPEAKER, WORKSHOP FACILITATOR, HOST OF IGNITING COURAGE PODCAST AND CREATOR OF FLOOR IT: POWER PRINCIPLES TO ACCELERATE YOUR LIFE.

After 20 years in highly successful leadership positions in various corporate settings, Anne founded Different Shoe Enterprises and now uses her experience, education, and expertise to ignite her audiences courage to embrace the uncomfortable; in change, in communication and in becoming influential with others. She shares fun and relevant stories, time-tested knowledge immediately applicable strategies for action, and by sharing her belief in everyone's ability to be stronger, to be better, and to live the successful lives they want.

A key asset Anne brings to her keynotes and interactive seminars is her wealth of varied experiences. Personally, and professionally, Anne has done a lot, from international marathons, animal training, winning a figure competition, volunteering at an elephant sanctuary and singing opera at a performing arts school. Through engaging and entertaining storytelling, Anne makes strong experiential connections to her points, planting seeds that remain in the minds of her audiences, igniting courage well beyond their time together.

She is proud to have worked with many companies including Under Armour, The New England Aquarium, the CFDA, Marriott Hotels, several government agencies, Ecolab, Shell Oil and Wells Fargo as well as many entrepreneur, women's and human resource associations and conferences. She is the assistant director of the longest running Rotary high school leadership conference and is the co-founder of a life changing women's empowerment conference called Breaking My Boundaries.

Anne has enthusiastically and passionately spoken with large and small groups both nationally and internationally. She is a proven leader, educator and motivator, and empowers people to catalyze powerful change in their lives by embracing those uncomfortable moments people might have turned away from in the past.

www.AnneBonney.com | **Anne@AnneBonney.com**
PODCAST: http://igniting-courage.buzzsprout.com
(OR FIND IT WHERE ALL GREAT PODCASTS ARE FOUND)